ITALY

Padua • Venice

• Vallombrosa

• Florence
• Arcetri

• Pisa

• Rome

BONNIE CHRISTENSEN

I, Galileo

ALFRED A. KNOPF
NEW YORK

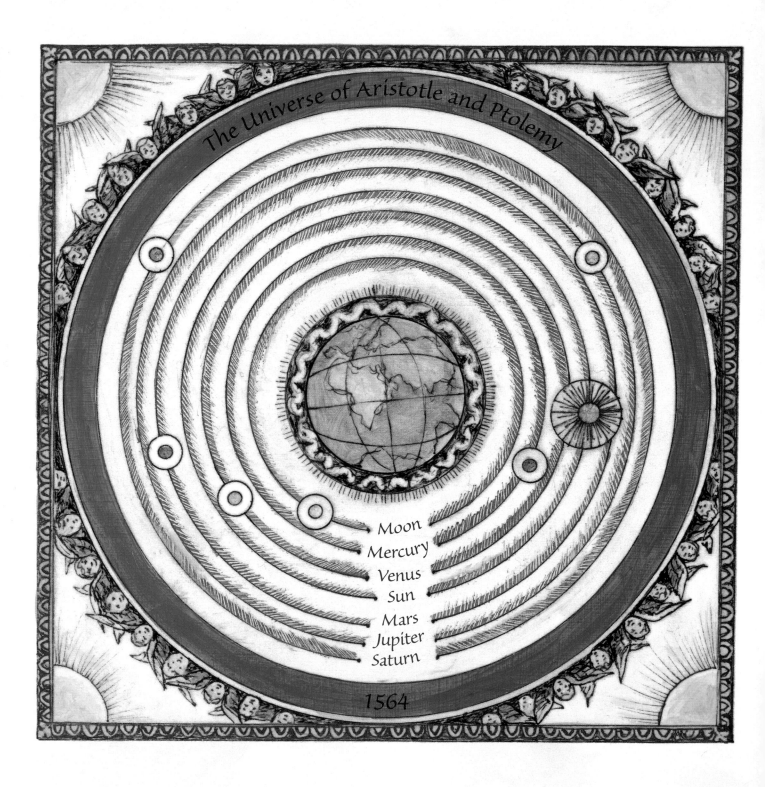

PREFACE

*I*magine a world with no clocks, thermometers, or telescopes. A world where everyone believes the earth stands still as the enormous sun travels around it once each day.

This was the world in 1564, the year of Galileo's birth. This was the world in which Galileo conducted scientific experiments by devising his own methods to keep time and measure distance.

Though Galileo believed his most important work involved moving objects, his real fame came from observing the heavens. No one had ever seen the surface of the moon, the phases of Venus, sunspots, or the moons of Jupiter—not until Galileo developed his telescope.

Through observation, experimentation, mathematics, and a great deal of ingenuity, Galileo made extraordinary scientific discoveries. The question was whether the rest of the world was willing, or ready, to listen.

I, Galileo Galilei, am old and can no longer see, but there was a time when I saw all the way to the stars—the moon, the planets, the sun. Their movements showed me a truth. A truth so profound it changed how we looked at the entire universe. A truth so unpopular it would get me into a world of trouble.

Now I am a prisoner, condemned to stay within these walls until the end of my days. I play the lute and listen for the nightingale's song to tell me night has fallen. Though I'm ending in darkness, I clearly recall the sun-filled hours of my early years.

I was the first child, center of my parents' universe. Life revolved around me. The lute tunes played by Father's students drifted in; light filled the room, then faded. As time passed, our family grew; noise and music echoed through our house in Pisa.

Season after season I watched the shadow of Saint Andrew's Chapel creep across the plaza and wondered why the shadow's shape changed a bit each day.

Father taught me music and mathematics and showed me how the two are joined—music theory! His revolutionary views challenged musical tradition and angered authorities.

"A person must be allowed to ask questions," he insisted, "and seek answers in search of truth."

At eleven, I was sent to the monastery at Vallombrosa for a formal education. The pious, scholarly life suited me, and so I decided to become a monk.

Father quickly put an end to that idea. Back to Pisa with me! An education in medicine at the university awaited, and a lucrative future as a doctor. Or so Father thought. Mathematics lured me, medicine bored me. After a few years and many disagreements, I left the university with no degree at all.

But like a clever cat, I landed on my feet. At my family's home, now in Florence, I helped Father with his musical experiments. I taught mathematics and gave public lectures, which proved very popular. So popular, in fact, that I was offered a teaching job at the University of Pisa. Yes! The same university I'd left without graduating.

Galileo and his father test how the length, tension, and thickness of a string affect the pitch of a note when the string is plucked.

I was not popular in Pisa, however. At the age of twenty-five, I scorned tradition. First by refusing to wear the cumbersome robes of a professor, then by disputing one of Aristotle's sacred laws of physics.

Aristotle, the famous ancient Greek philosopher, claimed a heavy object would fall faster than a light object. I disagreed. To prove my point, I dropped two cannonballs of different weights from the leaning tower. Just as I predicted, they fell at the exact same rate of speed. But the public was not convinced, even in the face of scientific proof. I was not invited to continue teaching at the University of Pisa.

In the winter of 1592, the University of Padua beckoned, with a better position and time for my own experiments. Back in Pisa, I'd observed a hanging lamp in the cathedral swinging back and forth. Each swing, like that of a pendulum, marked a unit of time. The memory of this inspired me to begin a great study of objects in motion, including the pendulum and its possibilities as a timekeeping device.

My star rose quickly in Padua and nearby Venice. The Venetian navy sought my advice on the most efficient placement of oars in their ships, and I invented an ingenious compass, a device capable of complex mathematical calculations, immensely useful to the military.

Yes, my compass was an extraordinary success, but nothing compared to what was to come.

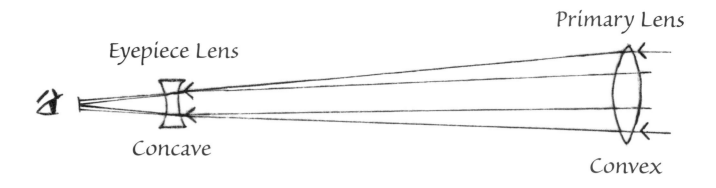

Eyepiece Lens

Primary Lens

Concave

Convex

Rumors were circulating through Venice of a new Dutch gadget—
a spyglass capable of magnifying distant objects. I seized upon the
idea and immediately began designing, calculating, and grinding
lenses for a far superior instrument. Within a matter of weeks, I held
in my hands the world's first truly scientific telescope.

The doge and senators of Venice eagerly climbed to the top of the
bell tower for a chance to look through my telescope. Through it they
saw tiny ships on the horizon—ships that would not be visible to even
the sharpest eyes for hours. They were astounded by my new creation.

But I was not satisfied with the magnification. I worked all
summer to increase the telescope's power.

Primary Lens

Eyepiece Lens

Then, one fall night, I lifted my telescope to the sky and viewed the moon.

Astonishing! Not the perfectly smooth moon Aristotle described, but a moon with peaks and valleys not unlike our Earth. And beyond . . . a seemingly infinite web of stars—and Jupiter! Jupiter aligned with four smaller celestial bodies never seen before.

For eight weeks I spent my nights in the cold, exploring the universe and making detailed sketches of my luminous, imperfect moon.

At the end of that winter, in 1610, I published my findings in *The Starry Messenger*. The book sold out instantly. All Europe was talking about the moon, Jupiter, and me. Suddenly I was as acclaimed as Christopher Columbus!

So acclaimed, in fact, that the grand duke of Tuscany, Cosimo II de' Medici, invited me to live in his court in Florence. At last, I could dedicate all my time to studying the heavens—to the exploration of strange spots crossing the surface of the sun and to the changing phases of Venus.

 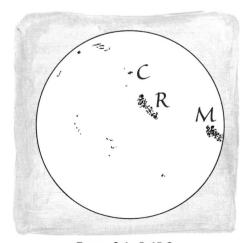

June 23, 1613   June 26, 1613

Galileo's observations of sunspots rotating with the sun on its axis raised the question:
Could Earth rotate on an axis, too?

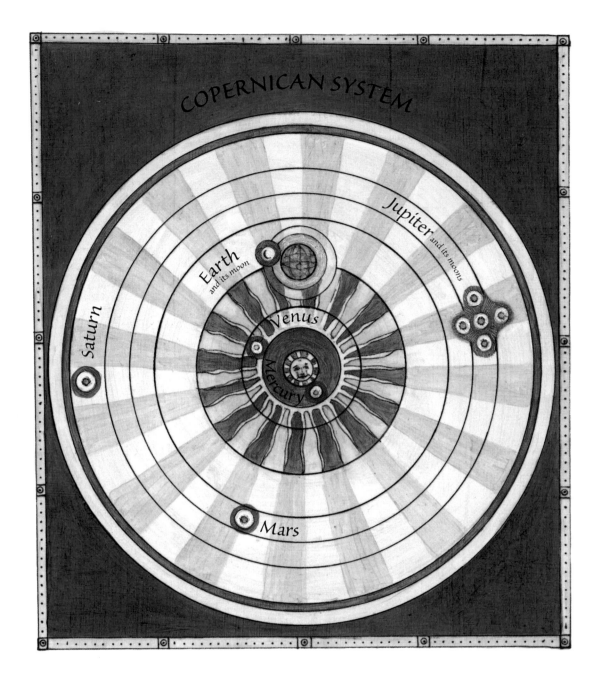

COPERNICAN SYSTEM

Saturn

Jupiter and its moons

Earth and its moon

Venus

Mercury

Mars

Through my telescope I saw the planets, sun, and moon. I also saw the truth—the sun is the center of the universe, with Earth and all the planets moving around it. My truth contradicted the popular belief that the sun, moon, planets, and all the stars circled a motionless Earth. Aristotle had proposed that theory nearly two thousand years earlier, Ptolemy refined it several hundred years later, and the Catholic Church continued to uphold it.

When poor Copernicus proposed a sun-centered universe, half a century before my birth, everyone laughed at him. But Copernicus had no way of proving his theory—no telescope.

With the telescope, I observed that Jupiter's four small celestial bodies, or moons, traveled around Jupiter, *not around the earth*, as everyone believed.

Later I recorded the phases of Venus. The number of phases, the existence of a full phase, and the distinct brightness of Venus proved it traveled around the sun, *not around the earth!* And if Venus traveled around the sun, so could the other planets, just as Copernicus had thought!

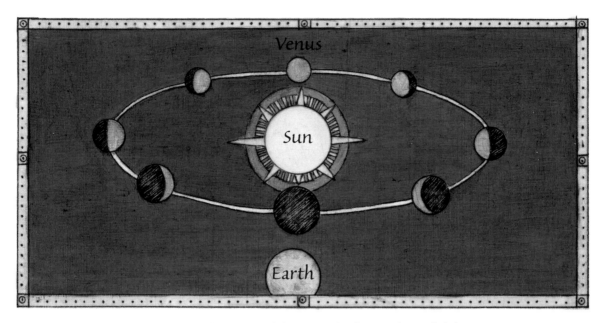

Venus revolving around the sun and reflecting the sun's light.

I wrote and lectured about Copernicus's sun-centered theory wherever and whenever I could. There were doubts and disbelief, even whispers that it was against the teachings of the Catholic Church. Heresy!

Then, in 1616, a church panel ruled that the very idea of a sun-centered universe *was* heresy. I was ordered to Rome and warned by the pope's representative to cease advocating the Copernican theory or suffer the consequences. I clearly recalled the consequences for Giordano Bruno, a follower of Copernicus, who had been imprisoned for seven years, then burned at the stake.

gnat   flea   moth

So for seven years I remained silent. I studied, wrote, and used
my lens-making skills to create the opposite of the telescope—the
microscope. Through my microscope I observed tiny creatures with
great amusement. The flea was horrible, but the moth and gnat were
quite beautiful. And particularly amazing was the way in which flies
could walk upside down on a mirror. Amazing, yes—but compared
to the sun, moon, and stars?

At last, a door opened. My old friend Maffeo Barberini became
pope. He called me to Rome and granted me freedom to write about
the sun-centered theory, but, he warned, only as an idea, not as
truth. Nothing could have made me happier. With renewed hope
and enthusiasm, I once again focused my attention on the heavens.

The plague doctor. His mask and clothing were meant to protect him from the plague.

For six years I labored on the *Dialogue on the Two Chief World Systems.*
I was often sick, and no longer young. How I longed for my book to be
finished, printed, and read. And for its arguments on a sun- versus earth-
centered universe to be discussed. But just as the book was ready for
printing, bubonic plague struck Florence, and the city came to a standstill.

Two years later, my book was finally published. It sold out immediately
in Florence, where it was met with delight and amazement.

But what of the copies sent to Rome? No word. I waited and worried.
Would the pope be pleased? Six long months passed.

Then I received the terrible news. A group of my enemies had convinced the pope I'd represented him as a fool in the *Dialogue*. Nothing could have been farther from my intent. Nevertheless, the pope was outraged. Distribution of my book was halted immediately.

The skies grew dark and closed in around me.

A month later, I was summoned to Rome to stand trial before the Church's Inquisition. My crime? Heresy and following Copernicus.

My sentence? Imprisonment for the rest of my days, within the walls of my house. All my writings were banned. The final blow came when the Inquisition posted copies of my sentence on walls throughout the cities of Europe. The humiliation was overwhelming.

So here we are. The truth and a blind old man locked away in the hills of Arcetri. The old man is a prisoner, but the truth? The truth has a way of escaping into the light.

AFTERWORD

Though Galileo was imprisoned at the end of his life, his ideas had taken root.

In time, other scientists, inspired by Galileo, proved he was right about the solar system, expanded his theories on moving objects, and improved his inventions.

Galileo's contributions were so vast that Albert Einstein called him "the father of modern science."

In 1992, almost four centuries after Galileo's trial, the Catholic Church officially admitted it had been wrong in condemning Galileo and that he had been right in declaring the sun the center of our solar system.

A statue of Galileo in the Uffizi Gallery in Florence.

CHRONOLOGY

1503 — Leonardo da Vinci paints the *Mona Lisa* in Florence, Italy.

1508 — Michelangelo begins painting the Sistine Chapel in Vatican City.

1519 — Ferdinand Magellan sets out from Spain to sail around the world.

1543 — Polish astronomer Nicolaus Copernicus publishes his sun-centered theory and dies shortly thereafter.

1552 — Books on geography and astronomy are burned in England because people think they contain magic.

1564 — Galileo Galilei is born on February 15 in Pisa.

1564 — English poet and playwright William Shakespeare is born on April 26.

1570 — Abraham Ortelius publishes the first world atlas, called *Theatre of the World*. It contains seventy maps.

1580 — Sir Francis Drake completes his circumnavigation of the earth.

1581 — Galileo enrolls in the University of Pisa, where he studies medicine and mathematics.

1597 — Galileo invents the geometric and military compass.

1599 — The Globe Theatre is built in London.

1602 — Galileo conducts experiments with the pendulum and time measuring.

1607 — Jamestown, Virginia, is founded by English colonists.

1609 — Galileo creates his telescope.

1611 — The King James Bible is published.

1616 — Pope Paul V warns Galileo to stop promoting the Copernican sun-centered-universe theory.

1618 — The Thirty Years' War between the Protestants and the Catholics begins.

1620 — The Pilgrims land at Plymouth Rock, Massachusetts.

1626 — St. Peter's Basilica in Rome is completed.

1632 — Galileo publishes *Dialogue on the Two Chief World Systems*. Pope Urban VIII (Maffeo Barberini) stops distribution of the book, and the case is referred to the Inquisition.

1633 — Galileo appears before the Inquisition in Rome. He is charged with heresy and given a life sentence under house arrest.

1642 — Galileo dies in Arcetri on January 8.

1642 — Isaac Newton is born in England on December 15.

1989 — NASA launches a spacecraft named *Galileo* to explore the moons of Jupiter.

1995 — The *Galileo* reaches Jupiter.

GALILEO'S EXPERIMENTS

FALLING BODIES — Galileo tested the speed at which objects of different weights fall. The first of these tests was done at the leaning tower of Pisa.

PENDULUMS — Galileo tested how the weight of the bob, the length of the cord, and the height of release affect the speed at which the pendulum swings.

INCLINED PLANES — Galileo tested the speed at which objects fall or roll down planes of different inclines. These experiments led to the concept of acceleration.

PROJECTILES — Galileo proved that objects of the same weight fall at the same speed whether thrown (projected) or dropped.

BODIES THAT FLOAT ON WATER — Galileo proved that objects floating on water are suspended because of their lighter weight, not because of their shape, as Aristotle believed.

GALILEO'S INVENTIONS AND IMPROVEMENTS

HYDROSTATIC SCALE — A device for weighing objects in air and water.

PUMP AND IRRIGATION SYSTEM — A means of raising water from under the ground for wells and irrigation.

GEOMETRIC AND MILITARY COMPASS — A pocket calculator that could easily calculate percentages, square roots, areas and volumes, and other mathematic and geometric functions.

THERMOMETER — An instrument for measuring air temperature.

TELESCOPE — Galileo improved a rudimentary spyglass invented in Holland by Hans Lippershey to the point that it could magnify distant objects thirty times. This improvement allowed him to be the first person ever to view the surface of the moon and the moons of Jupiter and to make numerous other astronomic discoveries.

MICROSCOPE — Galileo invented a system of lenses to magnify small objects. In 1676, Antonie van Leeuwenhoek of Holland improved the microscope so that it was capable of magnifying objects 270 times, making even tiny blood cells visible.

PENDULUM CLOCK — At the end of his life, Galileo described in detail the workings of a pendulum clock, but the project was not completed in his lifetime.

GALILEO'S ASTRONOMIC DISCOVERIES

THE SURFACE OF THE MOON — With his telescope, Galileo discovered that the surface of the moon was much like Earth's surface and not perfect, as believed by Aristotle and the Catholic Church.

THE FOUR MOONS OF JUPITER — Through ongoing observation, Galileo learned that the moons near Jupiter revolved around Jupiter, *not* Earth.

THE PHASES OF VENUS — After observing that Venus displayed many phases, similar to the moon's, Galileo concluded that Venus traveled around the sun and not Earth.

SUNSPOTS — Galileo observed the way in which sunspots moved across the surface of the sun over time, proving that the sun rotated on an axis and disproving the ancient idea that the heavens were perfect and unchanging.

GLOSSARY

ARISTOTLE — Greek philosopher (384 BC–322 BC) who wrote about natural sciences, physics, and metaphysics.

BUBONIC PLAGUE — Also known as the black death; a disease spread by rat fleas. In Italy, between 1629 and 1631, the bubonic plague killed 280,000 people.

DOGE — The elected leader of the former Republic of Venice.

GEOCENTRIC THEORY — The theory that Earth is the center of the universe. This view was originated by Aristotle, refined by Ptolemy, and upheld by the Catholic Church.

HELIOCENTRIC THEORY — The theory that the sun is the center of the universe, a concept first proposed by Nicolaus Copernicus in 1543.

HERETIC — A person who holds beliefs that are different from the established teachings of the Church.

POPE — The head of the Catholic Church.

PTOLEMY — A Roman citizen (AD 90–AD 168) who lived in Egypt and wrote in Greek. Ptolemy was an astronomer, mathematician, and geographer who developed complex mathematic models to support the idea of an Earth-centered universe.

SOLAR SYSTEM — The sun with planets and satellites revolving around it. This phrase did not exist until Copernicus's heliocentric theory was accepted. Before that, what we now call the solar system was described as the universe.

BIBLIOGRAPHY

Heilbron, J. L. *Galileo.* New York: Oxford University Press, 2010.

Panchyk, Richard. *Galileo for Kids.* Chicago: Chicago Review Press, 2005.

Reston, James Jr. *Galileo, a Life.* New York: HarperCollins, 1994.

Sís, Peter. *Starry Messenger.* New York: Farrar, Straus and Giroux, 1996.

Sobel, Dava. *Galileo's Daughter.* New York: Walker and Company, 1999.

WEBSITES

Galileo's Battle for the Heavens. NOVA. pbs.org/wgbh/nova/galileo

Galileo Portal. brunelleschi.imss.fi.it/portalegalileo/index.html

The Galileo Project. Rice University. galileo.rice.edu

Museo Galileo. www.museogalileo.it/en/index.html

FOR JANET SCHULMAN,
ANOTHER INDEPENDENT AND REBELLIOUS THINKER

WITH MANY THANKS TO LEDA FOR READING AND ANDREA FOR MODELING.

THIS IS A BORZOI BOOK PUBLISHED BY ALFRED A. KNOPF

Copyright © 2012 by Bonnie Christensen

All rights reserved. Published in the United States by Alfred A. Knopf, an imprint of Random House Children's Books,
a division of Random House, Inc., New York.

Knopf, Borzoi Books, and the colophon are registered trademarks of Random House, Inc.

Visit us on the Web! randomhouse.com/kids

Educators and librarians, for a variety of teaching tools, visit us at randomhouse.com/teachers

Library of Congress Cataloging-in-Publication Data

Christensen, Bonnie.

I, Galileo / Bonnie Christensen.

p.   cm.

ISBN 978-0-375-86753-8 (trade) — ISBN 978-0-375-96753-5 (lib. bdg.) [1. Galilei, Galileo, 1564–1642—Juvenile literature.
2. Astronomers—Italy—Biography—Juvenile literature. 3. Physicists—Italy—Biography—Juvenile literature.] I. Title.

QB36.G2C47 2012

520.92—dc23

[B]

2011025100

The illustrations in this book were created using a gouache resist with oil paints.

MANUFACTURED IN CHINA

June 2012

10 9 8 7 6 5 4 3 2 1

First Edition

Random House Children's Books supports the First Amendment and celebrates the right to read.